Twenty Minutes In Eternity

The story of Francis Robert Dumas;
the baby boy allowed to become a saint!

by Daniel P. Dumas

RED LEAD PRESS
PITTSBURGH, PENNSYLVANIA 15222

ISBN # 0-8059-8028-8
Printed in the United States of America

First Printing

For information or to order additional books, please write:
Red Lead Press
701 Smithfield Street
Pittsburgh, Pennsylvania 15222
U.S.A.
1-800-788-7654
or visit our web site on-line catalog at *www.redleadbooks.com*

In memory of my son, Francis, who taught us so much in such a short time.

In memory of my father, Robert A. Dumas, who passed away on the Feast of the Archangels, September 29, 2000.

In memory of our spiritual director, Fr. Robert E. Barber O.F.M., who passed away on August 16, 1999.

For those couples who may struggle with a similar cross, and the priests who guide them, that they do not lose hope.

For our friends, thank you for your prayers and support.

For my family, that you may never forget.

Foreword

Daniel and Kristine Dumas have lived through every parent's worst nightmare: hearing that their child will be born with severe defects. You are about to read their gripping story, told with all the anguish and struggle that accompanied them through the last five months of their son Francis' development. This story is important, as the author indicates, so that the world will know " we had a son named Francis whom we loved very much." It is also important in a number of other ways.

At a time in our society when people are most often judged by their appearance, this is a testimony to a love that does not depend on appearances. It will be a consolation to other parents who may feel powerless when confronting the illness or disability of their children. It will be a source of encouragement to those tempted to despair by situations in life that are deemed hopeless by those who have little faith. It will remind the members of the medical profession both of the healing that they can bring by their human interaction with their patients, as well as challenge them to view all their patients as persons first and illnesses second. Finally, it is a stirring declaration of faith in the value of every human person from the first moment of conception.

Daniel and Kristine know what it is to suffer for their beliefs. They also know what it is to suffer for the one they love. In both cases, they were willing to commit their lives for the sake of a child who was completely vulnerable and at their mercy. Through prayer and God's grace, they recognized that no good could come to them or their child by choosing to end the life of an innocent person, in their case, their son. We can admire their courage, their dedication, and their faith. It is my hope that their story, with all its tragic details and its inspiring outcome, will contribute greatly to fostering in our times a culture favorably disposed to life in all its weakness and in all its wonder. May the story of Francis' short life convince many other parents of the inestimable value of the children that God has shared with them, whatever their conditions of life may be.

Most Reverend Joseph J. Gerry, O.S.B.
Bishop of Portland, Maine

In their difficulties, may married couples always find, in the words and in the heart of a priest, the echo of the voice and love of the Redeemer.

- Humanae Vitae, #29

The most serious duty of transmitting human life, for which married persons are the free and responsible collaborators of God the Creator, has always been a source of great joys to them, even if sometimes accompanied by not a few difficulties and by distress.

- Humanae Vitae, #1

We are facing an enormous and dramatic clash between good and evil, death and life, the "culture of death" and the "culture of life". We find ourselves not only "faced with" but necessarily "in the midst of" this conflict: we are all involved and we share in it, with the inescapable responsibility of choosing to be unconditionally pro-life.

- Evangelium Vitae, #28

The problem of birth, like every other problem regarding human life, is to be considered, beyond partial perspectives – whether of the biological or psychological, demographic or sociological orders – in the light of an integral vision of man and his vocation, not only his natural and earthly, but also his supernatural and eternal vocation.

- Humanae Vitae, #7

The so-called "quality of life" is interpreted primarily or exclusively as economic efficiency, inordinate consumerism, physical beauty and pleasure, to the neglect of the more profound dimensions – interpersonal, spiritual and religious – of existence.

In such a context suffering, an inescapable burden of human existence but also a factor of possible personal growth, is "censored", rejected as useless, indeed opposed as an evil, always and in every way to be avoided. When it cannot be avoided and the prospect of even some future well-being vanishes, then life appears to have lost all meaning and the temptation grows in man to claim the right to suppress it.

- Evangelium Vitae, #23

It belongs to the Holy Spirit to rule, sanctify, and animate creation, for he is God, consubstantial with the Father and the Son... Power over life pertains to the Spirit, for being God he preserves creation in the Father through the Son.

- Catechism of the Catholic Church, #703

Even certain sectors of the medical profession, which by its calling is directed to the defense and care of human life, are increasingly willing to carry out these acts (abortion, euthanasia) against the person. In this way the very nature of the medical profession is distorted and contradicted, and the dignity of those who practice it is degraded.

- Evangelium Vitae, #4

Prenatal diagnosis, which presents no moral objections if carried out in order to identify the medical treatment which may be needed by the child in the womb, all too often becomes an opportunity for proposing and procuring an abortion. This is eugenic abortion, justified in public opinion on the basis of a mentality – mistakenly held to be consistent with the demands of "therapeutic interventions" – which accepts life only under certain conditions and rejects it when it is affected by any limitation, handicap, or illness.

- Evangelium Vitae, #14

The Church is close to those married couples who, with great anguish and suffering, willing accept gravely handi-capped children.

- Evangelium Vitae, #63

When death is clearly imminent and inevitable, one can in conscience "refuse forms of treatment that would only secure a precarious and burdensome prolongation of life, so long as the normal care due to the sick person in similar cases is not interrupted".

To forego extraordinary or disproportionate means expresses acceptance of the human condition in the face of death.

- Evangelium Vitae, #64

"I do not know how you came into being in my womb. It was not I who gave you life and breath, nor I who set in order the elements within each of you. Therefore the Creator of the world, who shaped the beginning of man and devised the origin of all things, will in His mercy give life and breath back to you again, since you now forget your-selves for the sake of His laws".

- 2nd Maccabees, 7:22-23.

Part of this daily heroism is also the silent but effective and eloquent witness of all those "brave mothers who devote themselves to their own family without reserve, who suffer in giving birth to their children and who are ready to make any effort, to face any sacrifice, in order to pass onto them the best of themselves".

In living out their mission "these heroic women do not always find support in the world around them. On the contrary, the cultural models frequently promoted and broadcast by the media do not encourage motherhood. In the name of progress and modernity the values of fidelity, chastity, sacrifice, to which a host of Christian wives and mothers have been born and continue to bear outstanding witness, are presented as obsolete... We thank you, heroic mothers, for your invincible love! We thank you for your intrepid trust in God and in his love. We thank you for the sacrifice of your life... In the Paschal Mystery, Christ restores to you the gift you gave him. Indeed, he has the power to give you back the life you gave him as an offering".

- Evangelium Vitae, #86

I

The Perfect Sign

I awoke December 19, 1997, to what I thought would be just another ordinary Friday. Laying my head down to sleep later that night, I realized I was not the same person who had begun the day. All my beliefs and convictions had suddenly been thrust into the greatest trial of my life. Every thought, emotion, and subsequent actions would have to be sifted, tested, and tried. Family, friends, and acquaintances would all play a part. Lives would be changed forever. Faith was to be the ultimate battlefield. Eternal souls would be the spoils.

My wife, Kristine, had a doctor's appointment that morning; a routine prenatal checkup. She was about sixteen weeks pregnant with our third child. We had high hopes that this pregnancy would be different from the previous two, which both had ended in emergency caesarean sections. Our goal was to have a healthy pregnancy followed by a natural delivery. Christmas, only a few days away, added to the excitement already present in the air.

I was at work, driving a garbage truck, when I was notified that my wife needed me to go to my parents' house as soon as possible. The fifteen-minute drive gave me plenty of time to conjure up all sorts of emergency situations. Could it be my mother or father? Could something have happened to my wife or children? I arrived to find my wife waiting for me, crying uncontrollably. My mother's eyes were full of tears as well. My father gave me his serious look, which I knew to be a precursor for bad news. My wife told me that her doctor could not find our baby's heartbeat. My wife was devastated. At that moment she believed our child was dead. The doctor had instructed us to go immediately to the hospital; there they would use ultrasound to try and locate the baby's heartbeat.

We had been overjoyed at the thought of welcoming our third child into our home. Now it seemed those dreams had been shattered. Kristine had felt this moment coming. Ever since she first found out she was pregnant she knew something was wrong. Physically she felt fine, but emotionally she felt she was not attached to this child, as a mother should be. She had told me she sensed something wasn't right and that it was preventing her from bonding with the developing life within her. She couldn't fully explain it to me, but it was there, an awful feeling. I tried my best to comfort her on the way to the hospital. I assured her that if our child had died, his soul would be with God, and we could have more children together.

I was silently praying "*Hail Mary...*" after "*Hail Mary...*" as the sonogram began. I felt I needed to remind the Blessed Mother of the joy she had at the birth of Christ. I didn't want our joy stolen from us by the death of a child. The tension in the air was almost overwhelming. The technician was trying to lighten the situation by being very outgoing, even attempting to slip in an occasional joke. Kristine, fearing the worst, remained silent, eyes glued to the ultrasound screen. I believe I saw a small ray of hope when she momentarily took her eyes off the monitor and quickly glanced at me. Our lives had now become spellbound to the outcome of that one sonogram.

Ten minutes of constant searching by the technician had finally succeeded in locating our child's heartbeat. Our baby was still alive! Relief flowed into the room. Kristine and I were elated. Her face once again took on the joyful glow of expectant motherhood. The feeling of relief was strengthened when we saw our child's beating heart. We were shown two arms, two legs, the head, and even the spine. The tech left the room twice to invite other sonographers to scan our baby. Never did we question why three technicians were performing an ultrasound. There were no indications that anything further could be wrong. The technician concluded the ultrasound by freezing the screen on an image of our baby's hand. Remarkably, our child was making a perfect sign of peace with his fingers. I immediately took it as a sign that he knew what we had just gone through. He was reassuring us that everything was going to be okay. He was still with us!

Relieved, we were led to a waiting room. The technician needed to call our doctor at his office and discuss the results of the ultrasound. Our doctor would then call us at the hospital to confirm the results. Confident in the fact that the ultrasound revealed our baby was alive, we decided that I should return to work to finish my day. I left Kristine alone by herself to wait for the doctor's report that our child was alive and well. Shortly after I began my route again, I was notified a second time about an emergency at my parents' house. I pulled the truck over at the nearest pay phone and called my mother. She could barely speak to me. She struggled to tell me it was serious and that I needed to get there quickly. I prayed continuously all the way there.

Nothing could ever have prepared me for the news that awaited. Entering the house, I found my wife in an almost hysterical state. She screamed out that our baby was severely deformed and had major physical abnormalities. I held her tight as she cried out in anguish, as only a mother can when her worst fears are realized. Life, as we knew it, had ended.

It took Kristine some time to explain all that had occurred since I left the hospital waiting room. She was crying as she told me how the technician had returned to waiting room and instructed her to go to our doctor's office. The doctor had suggested Kristine go to his office so he could speak to her in person. The technician never gave even the slightest indication that something could be wrong. My wife left the hospital and drove to the doctor's office excited that our baby was fine.

As our doctor entered the exam room, Kristine gave him the good news; the hospital had found the baby's heartbeat. 'Oh' he said, 'they didn't tell you anything? Kristine your baby has many birth defects.' He then proceeded to explain that after having reviewed the ultrasound, and having listened to the technician's report, he believed our baby had a severe, physical abnormality. His preliminary diagnosis was that our child had something called Potters Syndrome. He provided Kristine with some basic information on Potter's Syndrome to help her understand. The initial force of his words crushed Kristine deep inside. She bore the impact alone, and now had to inform her husband. Our doctor held her in his arms, and let her cry; creating a bond which lasted throughout the pregnancy.

II

The Incredible Journey

Our doctor referred us to specialists who handled high-risk complications on a daily basis. He suggested we take the weekend to come to grips with the situation we were in. He told us to talk it out with each other, with family and friends, and with our clergyman. He wanted us to let some of the shock wear off, or sink in, and then meet with the specialist on Monday. His advice was heeded and thus began our incredible journey.

My sister, upon hearing the news, immediately went on the Internet and found information on Potter's Syndrome. We learned that the kidneys do not develop properly for a child with Potter's Syndrome, causing an inadequate amount of amniotic fluid. The child's development is therefore stunted due to a lack of space. A mother's own organs will actually hinder her child's growth by pressing upon the uterus. We found out that most children with this affliction are usually male. We read how they never develop physically. Their facial features were described as being like a parrot's beak; the nose and mouth area failing to separate and form properly. To think our child may not even look human was an awful fear that remained constantly in our minds throughout the pregnancy.

My sister was able to locate a Potter's Syndrome support group on the Internet. She printed some testimonies from parents who had pregnancies diagnosed with this defect. I found it very disturbing that at least half of the people chose abortion as the way to solve their situation. In the pregnancies allowed to continue, half of the babies died in the womb before reaching term. Of the children who were actually born, the longest lived ten hours. Reading those letters helped break the ice, and enabled me to begin to accept the circumstances I had been thrust into. I tried to have Kristine read some of the more encouraging testimonies, but she wanted no part of any of them.

4

My wife felt cheated. Her child would be taken from her, stripped away by a defect she had never heard of before, and yet everyday there are women giving birth to unwanted children. Risking her life during the first two pregnancies was easily forgotten in the joy of holding a healthy newborn. She knew she was risking her life again if she continued with the pregnancy. She also knew any risk would be in vain. Her baby would die, and there was a possibility that she might die as well. She believed this pregnancy was for nothing. Bitterness had invaded her soul. Thoughts of having an abortion were prevalent. God, she thought, had abandoned her.

Everywhere around us were sights and sounds of the approaching Christmas Holiday, and yet we both felt removed from the world. The joy of Christmas could not even begin to penetrate the cloud of dark emotions that had encircled us. It took all our strength to wear fake smiles for the sake of our two children. Lauren and Peter were anxiously waiting for that special night. We knew they would not understand that which their parents could not comprehend. We tried our very best to be strong out front of them that weekend. Though neither one ever remarked, they saw their father as he cried for the very first time.

We attended Mass that Sunday at the local Franciscan monastery. The Monastery, as we called it, was a very special place for us. It was our spiritual home. Though we belonged to a parish near our home, it was this friary that truly fed and strengthened our spiritual lives. Our spiritual director, Fr. Robert, whom we met with regularly, lived there. When we first found out Kristine was pregnant, he had prayed over her, and blessed the pregnancy. Now we were returning to inform him of our dire circumstances. He knew right away, just by looking at us, that something was seriously wrong.

As I explained the situation to Fr. Robert, tears began to form in Kristine's eyes. He wrapped his arms around her, enveloping her within the brown Franciscan robe, and promised his constant support and prayers. Laying his hands upon her head, he prayed for her as a mother. Laying his hands on her stomach, he prayed for our unborn child. He prayed over us for the grace to accept God's providence in whatever may come our way. He offered a prayer of exorcism should we be spiritually attacked in our weakened state. He blessed us, and sent us on our way, with the knowledge that he would be praying for us.

Fr. Robert's counseling, and constant prayers, were a beacon of light that guided us through the stormy seas. I can look back now and see that Fr. Robert was a faithful servant whom God had deigned to be our foundation of strength. He became for us the voice of the Church.

III

The Truth of the Situation

Monday, December 22, 1997, three days after we had found out, we went to meet the high-risk pregnancy specialist. The mood was a combination of tremendous anxiety and unearthly fear. Our faces, drawn and expressionless, revealed our inner selves. We had wept together much of the weekend. The earth had stopped spinning; time was at a stand still. Today we would receive a definitive diagnosis. We would learn what was actually wrong with our baby.

I never expected a miracle, and I never doubted that God could perform one. I had come to understand, through reading the lives of the Saints, that the healing of a soul through suffering was far greater than any miraculous cure in the physical realm. Though I did not want to accept it, I knew in my heart that God would use this situation for the molding of our souls. We would be His instruments to reach out to others. I knew it would be too easy to have a miraculous healing. There would be no lasting effect. Christ crying out during the agony in the garden did not cause His Father to lessen the blow. I expected nothing less than all that we could handle.

Sitting in the waiting room that day I wondered what the problems could be to warrant the other mothers being there. I assumed that some were there because of their age. One woman needed crutches to walk, and I observed an emergency medical bracelet on another woman. All around us it appeared that mothers were there mainly for their own health reasons. We seemed to be the only couple that had medical problems with our baby. The small talk in the office was silenced as a noticeably mentally slow woman addressed Kristine from across the room. The woman innocently asked her how many weeks along she was. Kristine answered that she was sixteen weeks. The slow woman responded that she was only eight weeks along. The woman then told Kristine she wished she could switch places with her so she wouldn't have to wait as

6

long to hold a baby. Kristine abruptly, and very sharply, told her not to wish for that. A strong glare issued forth from Kristine to the woman. The gesture was well accepted; from then on the room remained silent.

I was praying for strength as the sonogram began. Deep inside I was hoping it was all just a terrible mistake. Maybe the technician would see that the first ultrasound had been wrong. Kristine was silent on the exam table, eyes fixed on the monitor. I sat beside her holding her hand. My body was shivering with nervousness. I felt very cold in the dimly lit, gray walled room. Kristine was motionless as the technician touched her stomach with the ultrasound wand. Ten seconds into the exam the technician confirmed that our baby had major physical abnormalities. I squeezed Kristine's hand as the blow swept across us. She glanced at me for a brief moment, and then fixed her stare back upon our baby displayed on the monitor. The technician proceeded to take us through the ultrasound, step by step, explaining everything she saw, whether it was good or bad.

The abnormalities made it impossible for the technician to locate and identify individually, any of the major organs. A large mass was visible, floating outside of our child's torso. The major organs were presumed to be what comprised this floating mass. The tech was able to show us that our baby had two arms and two legs. We were also shown about five major bends and twists of our baby's spine. Our child was severely deformed and contorted. The tech revealed that our baby's head appeared to be arched backwards, as if to see behind oneself. The chest was shifted towards the left, while the midsection and pelvis were shifted towards the right. The child was not in the fetal position but rather resting on his knees, on all fours. The lower legs and feet were folded up towards the child's back. The baby was said to be small for sixteen weeks gestation. The life shown to us on the monitor was unrecognizable as a human child, as our child.

The words of the technician slashed deeper and deeper into our very souls. It was not a mistake. It was not a dream. No one came in to wake us from this nightmare. The truth of the situation was infallibly set forth before us. I frantically searched my mind for encouraging words to tell my wife. Words of even the least comfort escaped me and I was forced to remain silent. My strength was being put to the test controlling my own emotions. I resigned to holding my wife's hand with a firm, yet trembling grip. I was helpless; unable to offer assistance to my own family. I quickly realized I had no control over the events that were happening.

Kristine closed her eyes as the monitor screen went black. The technician left the room to consult with the specialist, leaving us alone for what felt like an eternity. Incapable of speech, we shared our sorrow in a bond of silence.

IV

An All Out Offensive

Entering the room, the doctor and technician saved us from the embattling sound of silence. Having reviewed the ultrasound, the doctor informed us that our baby did not have Potter's Syndrome. Without hesitation she confirmed that our child had severe physical abnormalities. Our baby, we were told, had no chance of survival. She explained that what happened to our baby was extremely rare, and that a chance of a reoccurrence would be very low. No diagnosis was offered, other than we were victims of bad luck. Then doctor assured us that she would take care of everything and have us back to normal as soon as possible. The doctor, turning her back towards us, began scanning her appointment book for an opportunity to render the situation finished.

Kristine immediately sat up and very sternly told the doctor she did not believe in abortion. Chuckling as she turned back towards us, the doctor asked us who had put such ideas into our heads. My wife assured her that we had a priest acting as our spiritual advisor. I was stunned as the doctor proceeded to share her views of priests, and the Catholic Church. She quickly expressed her distrust of priests, and how unwise it is to listen to men in regards to female issues. She was proud of her twelve years of Catholic schooling and therefore, in her opinion, she knew the Church better than anyone. She believed that because the Church was not a woman, it had no right to tell women what they can and cannot do with their bodies. She continued to rant and rave about the Church and its ministers. I saw abortion rearing its ugly head through her, launching an all out offensive against our beliefs.

" Madam!" I quickly snapped back. "I am Roman Catholic and I do not believe in abortion! Life begins at conception and I will fight for my child's life until natural death!"

The doctor fell silent into shock upon hearing these words. The room was once again quiet as all present pondered what had just taken place. How absurd my response must have sounded to her. Her professional influence, and common sense, would tell anyone an abortion was the proper solution. I am sure we were labeled as religious fanatics at that moment. We had stood up to the evil and turned down the easy way out. The current of the world was flowing against us and yet we chose to cling to that rock, in the middle of the torrent, which was our faith. The doctor made it clear to us that we were now moving forward against her better judgment. Though she could not offer us any hope of life for our child, she would do what she could to help us through the pregnancy. These final words carried no consolation.

An amniocentesis was performed to reveal any possible genetic or chromosomal abnormalities. The test might give us a definitive diagnosis and maybe the risk of reoccurrence. Amniotic fluid was drawn from my wife's womb through a large needle inserted into her abdomen. Kristine experienced excruciating pain during the extraction. The results of this test would be known in about ten days. The findings would be reviewed and explained to us during a meeting with a geneticist.

As this traumatic office visit was drawing to a close, Kristine calmly asked the doctor if our baby would be born alive. The doctor did not expect our child to live to term, but she could not say for certain. Suddenly it struck me. Abortion had been her prescription for the hopeless cause only a few minutes prior. Now, she was admitting that the child could be born alive. Her quick solution was one of convenience. In reality I could be the father of a severely handicapped and deformed child. Having had little exposure to handicapped persons while growing up, I felt very uncomfortable around them. How would I feel towards my own child? Would I, could I love such a child?

Kristine and I left the office with the sad confirmation that our child had major physical abnormalities and deformities. The experiences in the exam room had taken our souls out of the world. I felt like I was looking in on all that was happening around me, while not being a part of it. Circumstances were happening and changing so quickly that nothing was able to fully register within us. The mask of the world had been torn off. This visit to the doctor had shown us a battlefield, abounding with traps and snares, not in our favor. Death was waiting to greet each footstep. I now could clearly see, as Christ had said, that the road to life would be narrow and hard to follow. I saw with spiritual eyes that I was nothing, and that this experience was greater than any preconceived idea I had of myself. Faith, a leap of faith, would be our only chance of crossing this battlefield. Hardly a word was said between Kristine and I, as we drove home from the office on that gray afternoon.

Kristine's next office visit with our family doctor enabled her to relate our experience with that particular high-risk specialist. He understood that the last thing we needed was a doctor against, and openly confronting, our sincerely held beliefs. Our doctor phoned the pregnancy center and discussed the situation with the senior physician, demanding that another doctor be assigned to our care. From then on we were able to see the other physician on staff for the remainder of our office visits. Our family doctor continued to see Kristine monthly throughout the pregnancy. He offered her medical, and emotional, advice and counseling. Kristine looked forward to her visits with him. He showed genuine sincerity for her physical and emotional well-being.

V

A Ray of Light

We returned to the high-risk pregnancy center in early January for the results of the amniocentesis, and another ultrasound. The amnio revealed that there was nothing wrong with the baby's chromosomes or genes. No definitive diagnosis could be given to us as to why this had happened, only that the situation was irreparable. An unknown cause was snatching the life of our child from us. It all felt so unfair.

The amnio also revealed that our child was a boy. Knowing the sex of our child began a deeper bonding. Our abnormal, deformed child was a little baby boy we named Francis Robert. He was given the name Francis after St. Francis of Assisi and the Franciscan Monastery that had led us to a deeper and more devout spiritual life. We gave him the name Robert in honor of my father, whom we saw as a great example of living faith. Robert was also the name of our spiritual director, who was our constant rock of strength. In giving his name we declared to the world the dignity of this unborn life. Francis Robert was not a tragic situation! Francis was our son!

The ultrasound performed that day once again confirmed the physical abnormalities as being incompatible with life. Our new doctor at the center advised us to take the pregnancy one day at a time. Nature would have to take its course. Nothing could be done medically to even possibly correct the birth defects. Though there was no real way to tell, the physician believed the baby would not make it past twenty weeks gestation. Kristine was assured that she would be able to tell if our son died within her womb. Reality became clearer while our hope disappeared in the dark cloud of despair. Shock, our constant companion, had once again strengthened the relationship. Our new doctor told us to "hang in there" and left the room.

We were ready to leave the exam room when the technician stopped us. She was the same tech who performed the previous ultrasound that had confirmed our child's abnormalities. She was the tech present when the former physician assigned to our care attacked our beliefs and promoted having an abortion. Kristine and I felt comfortable in her presence. Her honesty, even though it bore grievous news, was appreciated. She handed us her business card. Her eyes quickly welled with tears as she told us how remarkable she thought we were. She said she had never met two people like us before. She wanted us to contact her after the pregnancy to let her know how everything turned out. Our experience, she believed, would help her if confronted with another situation like ours. Her career, performing ultrasounds, and training others, had never exposed her to the gauntlet of moral and ethical questions our situation delivered. She embraced us both as we left the exam room.

I suddenly realized, as I pondered the event that had just happened, that God was working! He was touching people. I do not believe the tech had a profound religious experience, but I believe the Holy Spirit moved her to contemplate the faith Kristine and I had displayed. What this tech probably saw as a burst of emotion that let down her professional guard, I came to realize as God stirring the hearts of those who spoke to us of our child. I believe God reached out to a perfect stranger through our own suffering.

A different kind of joy, a contented joy, comforted me in knowing God was using our situation to call to others. Seeing God's work bring about genuine compassion, in a setting usually unsympathetic to the individual, revived in me a flame of hope. In a novice, yet sincere way, I began to understand why St. Francis of Assisi prayed to be a "channel" of His peace. A certain sense of peace envelops the soul when one's sufferings become a ray of light to another.

VI

Under the Cross

We knew we could not keep this devastating news to ourselves. Kristine and I decided to call some of our closest friends, who we knew to be devout Catholics, and ask them for their prayers. Relating the news over and over again made those the hardest phone calls I had ever made. Kristine did not make any calls herself; she sat silently next to me reliving the dreadful news. Little did I know this small band of prayer warriors would divide the bond of faith I shared with Kristine. I was looking at the situation with a spiritual and eternal perspective. Kristine appeared to be relying on a strictly temporal perception. It became apparent from our reactions to our friends' responses that we were not united as a couple in this struggle.

Our close friends had all viewed our distressing news from the spiritual perspective. We were told we were chosen by God to be an example for others. One friend said she couldn't think of two better people for this to happen to. We were told a blessing from God had been bestowed upon us; something major in the spiritual realm would certainly come of this pregnancy. All these themes, and similar other ones, were reiterated over and over again by the select few I chose to call that first day. Talking with my friends gave me strong feelings of support and encouragement. Though they could not fully share the weight of such a cross, they seemed to understand the magnitude of the situation. One couple stated they were honored that we chose to include them in our hour of sorrow.

Anger had settled deep within Kristine. Only recently we had struggled over the Church's teaching against contraception. It took us a year and a half to come to understand, and fully embrace, the Church's teaching put forth in the encyclical letter *Humanae Vitae*. We were practicing natural family planning. We were following the teaching of the Church. We were trying to do

13

what was right and yet received only sorrow in return. Kristine quickly became sick of hearing how blessed she was. The whole situation, she believed, was a case of bad luck.

She truly felt God had abandoned her. The entire pregnancy was useless and in vain. Kristine did not care about graces and merits; she wanted a healthy baby!

Indirectly, the idea of having an abortion was promoted to us by other family members and friends. Kristine, they said, should not put her health and safety in jeopardy. The best path would be to resolve the pregnancy before something serious happened to her. Kristine, well aware of her previous two serious pregnancies, showed some consideration of their pleas. Thankfully there remained in her the desire to follow Church teaching. Even though she desperately wanted a way out, she knew abortion was intrinsically evil. I knew I needed to be strong at all times to support my wife through this. I placed myself at the foot of the Church. I would make no decisions alone, but rather, only in the light of Church teaching. Under no circumstance, no matter how grave, would I do other than what the Church prescribed.

This interior pledge of submission to the Church gave me the strength and freedom to suffer this cross. For me, I felt at ease. I knew I was doing what was right. I stopped thinking of future events and began accepting what each passing hour brought forth. My accepting demeanor seemed to anger Kristine. She was struggling within a whirlwind of thoughts and emotions. She felt she had the heavier cross to bear because she had to suffer both physically and emotionally. She began to resent the way I was handling the situation. I always knew she would suffer a pain greater than mine, yet I also knew we were walking under the same cross. I was to become Simon, the support throughout our personal way of the cross.

VII

Day In Day Out

Cards of sympathy and petitions of prayers were often met with the same resentment that overshadowed the remainder of the pregnancy. Kristine thought these gestures to be meaningless. It is too easy to send a card or offer a prayer if you are not the one trying to handle the crisis. Positive support from friends and family, myself included, actually seemed to make Kristine close in more around herself. Our spiritual director, Fr. Robert, was the only person Kristine viewed as being of any spiritual support. Rather than gloss over the situation with what she thought to be shallow words of grace and blessing, he listened to her, and acknowledged her greatest fears as possible truths. Kristine wanted to deal with the present physical reality. Myself and others were trying to view everything in the assurance of God's grace.

The foundation had been created. We had begun this journey by taking different roads that seldom crossed. We often found it hard to meet in the middle. To those around us we seemed at times to be lacking all emotion and expression. Our daily routine became the secret weapon that held us together. Life outside of our tragic news was monotonous and mundane. How simple and meaningless life would be without this cross. Each in our own way we were plodding along towards the place where neither of us wanted to be. In five to six months our journey would end, but how?

Unanswered questions and strong feelings of doubt plagued Kristine throughout the pregnancy. Why should she carry this child and continue the pregnancy? The baby was going to die anyway. Would the baby die within her womb? Would she have to carry and deliver a dead baby? Would the child die during the birth process? Could our child live for several minutes, days, months, or years? What about her own health? Could she still have more children? Would her uterus withstand natural childbirth after two cesarean sections? Would it rupture and bring about her death? Were two young children going to be left without a mother? These thoughts saturated her waking moments as well as her dreams.

Certain specific fears weighed the heaviest on Kristine. First, she feared our child would not look human. She feared that his face would be so grotesquely deformed that she would not be able to look at it. Secondly, Kristine feared looking into our baby's eyes. She knew that looking into our helpless, dying child's eyes would break down every defense she had. Kristine also feared hearing our child cry. The sound of a child's cry after birth is usually a sign of life; for our child it would herald his death. Finally, she did not want to watch and listen as her child died. Hanging like shadows in a darkened room, these fears surrounded Kristine with despair.

I frequently reminded Kristine how much our baby was depending on us. The world of perfection was against our abnormal child from the beginning. The only true love this child could ever feel in this world would pour forth from his parents. Born alive our child would need to feel the loving arms of his mother holding him safe. Anything less would be to leave the child scared and alone in the unforgiving world.

Common everyday situations added weight to the fear, the doubt, and the cross. One doesn't think twice about asking a pregnant woman when her baby is due, or asking about the excitement they must surely be feeling. Second nature forces congratulations to be showered upon the expectant mother. The blossoming tummy is always the focal point of any encounter with a pregnant woman. The joys of expectant motherhood are to be flaunted and encouraged on the mother to be. For this purpose was woman made, to give all the gift of life! The truth of the matter is that before one experiences the full joys of motherhood, she must first experience suffering and pain.

Kristine offered very little, if any, of her own personal feelings and struggles. She felt no one knew what she was going through. She felt people tried to trivialize, and play down the seriousness of the situation. It was not long before Kristine became tired of what she saw as shallow sympathy being thrust on her by those who had never suffered. Frequently people would offer their own success stories of accepting a miscarriage to try and comfort her. Kristine did not see the proposed parallel. Many times she told me she had prayed for a miscarriage so she would not have to face her haunting fears. Our friends and neighbors were all enjoying healthy pregnancies of their first, second, third, and fourth child. Though she was sincerely happy for them, Kristine found no one to whom she could truly relate.

We had come across a statistic, in a book on crisis pregnancies, which stated that 95% of all pregnancies, diagnosed with major abnormalities or birth defects, ended in the aborting of the child. This statistic was from the mid-eighties. We figured the percentage of aborted children must be even greater, if it were possible, during our crisis of 1998. Kristine had every right to feel alone in the world, few people had decided to follow this narrow path. Many of the people around us began to avoid mentioning, or even acknowledging the pregnancy. Some of those closest to us, including members of our immediate families, became silent. A strong feeling against the indifference of others fed the anger and bitterness Kristine was harboring.

Within our home the tension and anxiety levels were constantly high. Any little thing could trigger an explosive negative reaction. Unfortunately, we very often took out our frustrations on each other and our children. It was a very hard time for our whole family. Kristine and I didn't do well being alone. Someone else needed to be there to disrupt the constant worrying that plagued us night and day. Though we continued in our Catholic faith, attending Mass, family prayer, and regular spiritual direction, we had lost most of the deep joy our faith life had brought us. Our home became like a prison with four walls and an unchanging view. We faced each dreadfully long day one hour at a time.

VIII

Alone in our World

Expectant parents put much time and love into preparing their new baby's nursery. Shopping for a new crib, the perfect stroller, and that special first stuffed animal, adds to the joy and excitement of welcoming home a new baby. Friends and relatives do their best to surprise the soon-to-be mom with a baby shower. The joy and excitement is shared as it overflows to all those who seek out just the right gift for the budding family. Dad anticipates upholding the tradition of passing out cigars to celebrate his new child's arrival. Mom desperately tries to make up her mind on which outfit the baby will wear home from the hospital. Coworkers start an office pool to guess the date and time of the baby's arrival. A couple's whole world joins them at the greatest moment of their lives.

Kristine spent several days calling and meeting with funeral directors. Instead of looking for a new crib, she pondered over the styles and choices of infant caskets. A stroller, for lazy walks in the park, was not needed, but a final resting place was. Thankfully, a local Catholic cemetery donated to us a plot within the baby range, as it was called. That first stuffed animal gave way to the perfect flower arrangements for the funeral and burial. The special coming home outfit was now a white burial garment. There were no gifts from friends or relatives. There was no baby shower. Cigars remained unsold on store shelves. Coworkers very rarely even approached the subject. We were alone in our world.

In the midst of everything, the preparations for Francis' death kept our minds occupied. A local pastor opened the doors of his church to us for the funeral. It was the same church in which we were married, my wife was baptized and became Catholic in, and our first two children were both baptized there. This church had that deep special feeling of home, which gave us comfort. Our spiritual director felt honored to be the celebrant at the funeral. Some people came forward and offered financial help with the preparations. Relief came to us in knowing we were ready, at least in the temporal realm, for the death of our son, Francis. Several months still remained before the expected due date. Inside we were both trying to rush the outcome. An event happening soon would be easier to handle than what may happen later, or so we felt. Kristine frequently expressed her wish that it would all just come to an end.

The specialists had told us that it was highly unlikely Kristine would ever feel the baby move. His spine, they believed, was so deformed that it surely had damaged the spinal cord, preventing any movement of his arms or legs. Francis proved them wrong. He could move, and Kristine could feel him! The movements were not the strong kicks of a healthy child. Kristine described the feeling as a gentle fluttering, or soft tickle. She felt this movement just about everyday. As Francis grew, and the pregnancy progressed, these movements strengthened and reaffirmed the bond between mother and son. Kristine's fear of becoming attached was causing a deep emotional struggle within her. The more Francis became present to her, the greater her worries and fear. After all she would have to go through, she knew our son was still going to die. The wall of anger she had created to prevent herself from being attached to the baby was now crumbling away. Her love and concern for her child were more powerful.

Supermarkets and department stores provided many moments of sorrow. Kristine looked pregnant and had that angelic glow all expectant mothers possess. Many of our friends and acquaintances that we met at these public places had no idea what we were going through. Their well-intended inquiries into the presumed joyous occasion only drove the sword deeper into our hearts. People would offer us their congratulations and in return we would inform them that our child would not live. Instant shock and then a quick gesture of sympathy was the most common reaction. Most people were left speechless, fumbling with their inability to use the right words. No one knew what to say upon hearing such news. I became rather adept at rescuing the awkward from the situation. I asked for their prayers, not their words, to give us the strength to persevere.

Reactions were at times very cold. There were some people who seemed unmoved and indifferent to our news. Many people became silent. A cold shoulder would be thrown our way as they tried to avoid the subject. The people who disagreed with our decisions we could handle; it was those who ignored us that really hurt. Kristine wasn't invited to any baby showers. Mentioning pregnancy, babies, and all other subjects associated with the birth of a child, were mistakenly seen as bad taste. Our friends who were having children, or had babies, seemed uncomfortable at times being around us; afraid that something they might say or do would be upsetting to us.

The various responses people gave to us were very interesting to me. I found myself studying their reactions. Through these encounters I learned a lot about what it means, and how important it is, to have a life built on faith. I felt sorry for those people who could not even begin to comprehend the moral, ethical, and spiritual concerns that were blatantly presenting themselves. A couple women, evidently without thinking, asked us if we had found out to late to have an abortion. I discovered just how far away from the Truth this world could be. I offered small prayers for those people who held beliefs contrary to the teachings of the Church. I prayed, and thanked God for those people who supported us. The tide of our spiritual battle surged and fell with each person with whom we conversed.

Eventually the continuous telling of our story became too much for Kristine to bear. We stopped telling people the expected outcome of the pregnancy. We revealed only the due date and how excited we were to be having another child. After one of these brief encounters, my daughter Lauren asked me if we were lying by not telling the whole truth.

We remained grounded on our course by listening to our spiritual director constantly echoing the teachings of Christ and His Church. Fr. Robert's nightly phone calls were the beacon to which we looked for guidance. Though we were surrounded, and yet alone, in a sea of endless voices, Fr. Robert was always able to find a way into our hearts.

IX

His Name is Francis

Kristine and I would lie in bed, in the quiet of the night, and review each hour of every day. We contemplated the day's events and the different people with whom we spoke. We critically analyzed each hour to judge how well we were coping. We discussed the reactions and responses of others versus what we had told them. We shared new insights into the situation as well as new fears. Eventually Kristine would tell me about a little baby she happened to see during the day. Her voice would fill with that motherly joy as she described how cute a baby he was. The silence that followed always led to the hardest of all questions – Why? Why does my baby have to die? I cradled my wife and remained silent, enveloped in the soft cries of a grieving mother. Those nights were so very long.

People often referred to Francis, especially by those whom we met in the medical profession, as "it". Pronouns of a human nature were seldom used. Impersonal language terms were the norm, such as: it, fetus, and condition. I became disgusted at the lack of dignity afforded to my son. On the advise of our family doctor, Kristine and I wrote a statement of our belief and intent which we then distributed to all medical personnel handling our care.

This small letter was personally distributed to every doctor and nurse we met. I made sure that every file at every office we visited contained this letter. I wanted the world to know that we had a son named Francis whom we loved very much. Care providers started catching themselves using forms of impersonal speech and began referring to him as Francis. One neonatologist praised us for taking a stand. He wished more people experiencing crisis pregnancies had such strong faith. Our letter, he stated, inspired him.

ATTENTION: ALL CARE PROVIDERS

FROM: DANIEL AND KRISTINE DUMAS

RE: Our baby has been diagnosed to have major, physical abnormalities. These abnormalities are incompatible with life.

His name is FRANCIS ROBERT DUMAS!

If he is born alive we want to hold him immediately, and then thereafter. If he is stillborn we want to hold him.

We do not want any extraordinary means provided to prolong his life. Means to reduce suffering will be discussed at that time.

We want him photographed, just like a healthy baby, whether or not he is born alive.

We would like his footprints if possible.

We have a white garment we would like him clothed in before the undertaker claims his body.

We are practicing Roman Catholics and ask that a priest be notified.

Signed and dated.

X

Waters of Chaos

Shock, which had accompanied us through Christmas, had given way to deep spiritual and emotional battles by the time the Easter season was upon us. In my heart I sensed that Easter would not bring a great physical healing to Francis, though many people were praying vigorously for such an event. I was beginning to understand Easter in a far different way than I had ever before. Easter gives to mankind a guaranteed promise of Eternal Life. It was this promise I wanted for my son, for all my family.

Francis, if he were miraculously healed, would have to live out his life in this world. Therefore, I reasoned, there was a chance he could lose his soul through sin, and condemn himself to an eternity in Hell. Suffering and dying as an infant, he would be eternally in the presence of the Father. I looked towards Easter for my son's death while others continued to pray for his life.

I may have been thinking these issues out to deeply, or maybe trying to justify why this was happening, but the Easter promise grounded me to be able to look beyond this temporal realm. Easter had given me the assurance and strength to continue. The Easter season soon saturated me with spiritual insights I had never before probed.

Holy Mass became an ocean of inspiration to me. I no longer just went to Mass, but rather, I began to participate in, and experience the Mass. The Liturgy of the Word gave me countless reasons to stand fast in my faith. Doubts and worry were quickly driven away from me by the messages of the Gospel. The Word was making sense. I no longer heard the readings. I now anticipated listening to the Word of God. The Liturgy of the Eucharist drew me deeper into the essential Truth of our Faith. God was with us. He was giving of Himself for us. Suffering was becoming less of a burden and more of an invitation to participate in the cross. I felt great peace while at Mass. I was in my Father's house and he was taking care of me.

One particular verse of the Nicene Creed we profess during Mass jumped out at me each time I recited it. We profess to ' believe in the Holy Spirit, the Lord, the Giver of Life'. My son Francis was not some freak occurrence, disease, or syndrome. Francis was created and sustained in his mother's womb by the power of the Holy Spirit, the Giver of Life. The Holy Spirit caused and allowed my son to be. During the Profession of Faith I always prayed for the Holy Spirit to watch over this defenseless child to whom he had given the gift of life. As the Spirit of God hovered over the waters of chaos at the creation of the world, I prayed that he would be over the waters of chaos in my wife's womb.

I made frequent visits to the Blessed Sacrament. I usually went after a ten or twelve hour day in the rubbish industry. I was tired, dirty, and usually carried the day's odors of trash drippings on my clothing. My external appearance often reflected my inner battle. I would tell the Lord all that was going on in my life, in my heart, and in my mind. In the presence of our Lord I was able to unload the heavy burdens I could not share with the world. Kneeling before the Blessed Sacrament never produced any great insights, and never gave me easy answers to my multitude of questions. Our Lord's presence, humbled in the Blessed Sacrament, helped to calm the turmoil. I would leave the adoration chapel knowing that Christ was with me, even if the outward appearance seemed otherwise.

XI

To Sift Mere Words

Two years prior to the news that Kristine was pregnant with Francis, I had consecrated my life to the Blessed Mother. Consecrating my life according to the method and theology of St. Louis de Montfort, I gave myself, body and soul, all my possessions, my family, and the value of all my good actions, past, present, and future, to Our Lady for her to use for the greater glory of God. At the time I did not understand how one could give their family for God's greater glory. I assumed a child accepting a religious vocation was what St. Louis had in mind when asking us to give back to God.

Was I being called to sacrifice my son to God just as Abraham was called to give back Isaac? I felt as if my consecration was being tested to sift mere words from true faith. Allowing Francis to live his life, and relying on God to author his life, created an example of giving to God that which is always His; power over life and death. If I would lose my son to death, through faith, our Father would give him eternal life in Heaven.

Kristine kept much of her inner struggles of faith to herself. She felt even I, her husband, would have trouble understanding and relating to her personal experience. She revealed little of her inner spiritual life during the pregnancy. One could see she was engaged in a battle with Hell on Earth. Her face seldom bore a true smile, tainted by what troubled her deep inside. Her eyes were often far off, deep in anguished thoughts. Only the time spent in confidence with our spiritual director could lift her from this abyss. Fr. Robert's counsel renewed and invigorated her strength, enough to make it another day. The lingering question, 'Why?', continued its daily taunts.

Our regular visits to the high-risk pregnancy center had, by the beginning of the eighth month, become weekly. The doctors were diligently watching for the slightest sign of preeclampsia, or pregnancy induced hypertension. Kris and I were very worried that preeclampsia would develop again and complicate even more an already serious matter. We were relieved when the urine tests came back with only trace amounts of protein. With the due date of June 8th looming on the horizon, we were well aware the greatest struggles were yet to be fought.

Halfway through the eighth month, the specialists handling our care decided to perform another sonogram. The test was to check on Francis' growth and position for a possible delivery. A new technician was to perform the ultrasound that day. I believe he was not aware of Francis' abnormalities, or if he was aware of them, he was not prepared for what he saw. Once the sonogram was started and the first pictures appeared on the screen, the tech became very silent. We asked him questions about Francis, which he didn't, or couldn't answer. The tech became visibly frustrated while looking for anything of normality to measure. The standard items such as the bladder, the liver, and the lungs were unable to be singled out among the large, free-floating mass. Several attempts at measuring the spine and limbs were met with failure. After a quick three minutes of vain attempts at calculations, the tech abruptly left the room to consult with a physician. He never returned. The doctor came in to the room and went directly to the ultrasound machine. Apologizing, he quickly turned it off. Sonograms, in our case, he stated, would no longer be necessary. I knew from then on the medical profession had given up all hope. Only a divine intervention could help Francis now.

Two weeks prior to her due date Kristine's urine tested positive for a large protein spike, one of the first signs of the onset of preeclampsia. The doctor explained to us that we needed to bring this pregnancy to a conclusion as soon as possible to protect Kristine's health. No one ever thought that Francis would live past twenty weeks gestation, let alone make it all the way to term. We had not prepared ourselves for this situation. We now had the choice of clinically ending the pregnancy, or waiting about two more weeks for nature to run its own course unimpeded.

Francis, if he were a physically healthy child, had an almost 100% chance of living if born two weeks early. However, in the truth of reality, if the pregnancy continued for a couple more weeks it would have no bearing on the final outcome for our son. Francis' deformities and abnormalities were incompatible with life. Continuing the pregnancy to term would be detrimental to Kristine's own health. To conclude this pregnancy two weeks early would prevent her from developing a serious, and possibly fatal medical condition. After discussing our options with our doctor, and contemplating the moral questions involved, we, in good conscience, decided to bring the pregnancy to a conclusion.

XII

Alone in the City

On the morning of May 27, 1998, I brought Kristine to the hospital to begin the induction. The first procedure was to apply a gel to the cervix to help prepare it for its role in the birth process. When the application was finished, the doctor told us that it helps the process if you get up and walk around. We ended up leaving the hospital and walking around in the city for most of the afternoon. We both found our quiet walk together to be very relaxing, yet we also realized that the most major event of our lives was beginning to unfurl. While sitting on a sidewalk bench watching traffic and pedestrians rush about, I remember thinking how everyone was oblivious to the struggle that this expectant couple on a city bench were enduring. We were alone in the city, yet closer to one another than ever before. Together this young couple of faith would move mountains. That afternoon together prepared us for what lay ahead. Our son Francis would soon be born.

Kristine was admitted to the hospital that night because of pregnancy induced hypertension. The hospital was originally going to allow her to go home for a good night's rest and then return in the morning. High blood pressure forced her to become a patient. Magnesium was begun intravenously to help keep Kristine's blood pressure in check. The magnesium made her feel groggy and nauseous, and produced a nagging headache. The next morning, May 28th, with the help of intravenous drugs, the induction was vigorously promoted. It was only a matter of a few hours when Kristine's water broke, ushering in full-fledged labor pains. The waves of pain and contractions continued throughout the day and into early evening. I could do little more than hold her hand and wipe her face with a cool cloth. The intense pain of the contractions, together with the magnesium, caused her to vomit several times. Kristine, who had wanted as few drugs as possible, succumbed to the pain and agreed to intravenous morphine injections. I held her hand tight as her body drifted between rigid pain and limp exhaustion. My wife was enduring the battle of her life.

The morphine was having little effect on the induced pain Kristine was suffering. The nurse suggested an epidural, an injection directly into the spinal cord, as the best and last chance for controlling the pain. Kristine was well aware of the serious risks involved with an epidural, and was afraid of the idea of not being able to feel her body. The induction continued, without the epidural, late into the evening. As the midnight hour approached, Kristine had suffered through almost sixteen hours of induced labor. She gripped the padded bed rails tight with each wave of intense pain. Her body was not cooperating with this forced labor. I knew she just wanted everything to be over. She had had enough. Together we decided she had no other option than to accept the epidural.

XIII

Continue the Battle

I was asked to leave my wife's hospital room while the anesthesiologist performed the delicate procedure. They could not risk the chance of me bump-
ing him, making my wife move, or whatever other situation could arise. I
found myself walking the quiet, darkened halls of the hospital at 12:30 a.m.
I walked into a waiting room amid dead silence. I was alone. A single, small
table lamp lightened the room. The windows encircled me like blackened
mirrors against the dark night sky. I could see the deep anguish of the man
as I stared back at the reflection. Doubt enveloped my soul as never before.
Were we doing the right thing? What exactly was at stake? I was angry with
myself for putting my wife through this. I was even angrier with God. Where
was He in all His greatness and glory?

I had come to a point of helpless desperation. The realization that I was
not in control of the situation ate down to the core of my being a husband
and father. I needed to help my wife; I needed to save my son. My faith disappeared into the blackness outside that waiting room. After sixteen hours of
watching my wife suffer I had lost sight of God. Just as Christ had cried out
on the cross, I too cried to God at His abandonment. I had lost my grip on
the end of the rope. I had tried my best to hang on, but this cross had worn
me down. I prayed to God, out of anger, to pick me up, to stand in my place.
I demanded that God give me a physical sign to show me that what we were
doing was right. I wanted Him to prove that He was with us. I pleaded for
the strength to continue the battle.

I sought forgiveness for the anger in my heart as I walked the quiet halls
back to my wife's room. I was relieved to find Kristine resting comfortably in
her bed. The pain had vanished; the epidural had gone smoothly. The nurse
urged us to both try and get some sleep. I pulled up a chair and covered up

with a small blanket. Kristine closed her eyes still waiting for the inevitable. The nurse remained in the room, monitoring Kristine, and doing paperwork under a small light. Sleep escaped us both.

Half an hour had passed when suddenly the pain returned. Once again Kristine cried out in excruciating pain. Her knuckles became white, on the verge of splitting, as once again she gripped the bedrails. She curled tightly up in the fetal position in a failed attempt to cope. Her cries pleaded for anyone to make it stop. She laid there for an hour and a half suffering from the intense rhythmic pains. I sat by her side trying to do anything that might help. I felt totally useless.

Two hours after the epidural, the anesthesiologist came to her room and gave Kristine, what I came to call, a booster shot. A needle, similar to an I.V. had been left in her back. The anesthesiologist simply gave her an injection of the pain-killing drug through this devise. The pain subsided almost instantly. Kristine became limp with relief. Her reprieve was short lived as the pain returned within half an hour. The booster shots could only be given at a minimum of two-hour intervals. Kristine had to pay an hour and a half of pain for a half hour of relief. The nurse had mentioned that usually one booster shot would be sufficient to last until the birth. Kristine received a second, third, and fourth booster shot, to no avail. Her pain could not be breached.

Words cannot express our physical and emotional states after the last booster was administered, and failed, around 8:00 A.M. that morning. All we wanted was another child. We never dreamed we would have to endure so much and not receive that precious gift. Kristine was beyond exhaustion. She fell asleep in between the painful contractions that were continuing about four or five minutes apart. She was only dilated about six centimeters. After more than twenty hours of torturous contractions we both knew she was still far away from delivery. The nurses continued to monitor Francis, whose heart beat remained strong and regular. Though the little guy continued to defy all the medical prognostications, I was really scared my wife would not have the strength to survive until the birth. Would I need to summon a priest to administer to her the last rites? How would this nightmare end? Where was God?

XIV

Chasing a Rainbow

The nurses' shift change that morning brought us a small amount of relief. A nurse who had been with us all the day before was reassigned to my wife for that day. We felt close to her because she took the time to talk with us and seemed to have a deep and sincere affection for us. All the nurses at the hospital were exceptional throughout our stay, but this one nurse became a friend. She promised to stay by our side until Francis was born, no matter how long it took. Looking back it is very easy for me to see the tremendous difference this one nurse made. Her positive attitude, and her angelic demeanor, kept Kristine and I focused on what we had to do. She was truly our special nurse.

The pain and contractions continued throughout the morning. Kristine's speech became incoherent at times. She was so exhausted she was in a state of semi consciousness. I had never seen a person suffer so much for so long. It was horrible just having to watch it. The contractions remained four to five minutes apart, lasting approximately thirty to forty-five seconds. The doctor examined her around 11:00 A.M. and decided the induction had gone as far it could. Kristine had finally dilated a few more centimeters. Normally the hospital would have recommended a cesarean section much earlier, but Kristine was adamant against one. She had already had two cesarean sections and wanted to have this child naturally. The doctor gave Kristine the go ahead to start pushing. I tugged on my brown scapular in anticipation of much needed help.

Our special nurse took the time to explain to Kristine how to push during a contraction and rest in between them. We had never experienced a natural birth before, only emergency cesarean sections. The doctors had already explained to us that the baby would not be able to help with the delivery because of his abnormalities. Our nurse went over every aspect of the process with us, in advance of, during, and after each event. Finally we could see a light at the end of the tunnel. The pain Kristine felt became more endurable when she started pushing. She was no longer on her side clenching the bedrails; she was sitting up working to deliver her son. Kristine tried her best to give three strong pushes during each contraction. Her contractions remained four to five minutes apart forcing her to tediously wait for the opportunity to push. Groggily she pleaded for it to be over.

I looked around the room, while Kristine slept between contractions, and realized we were alone with our special nurse. I wondered where the doctors and other nurses were. I figured we probably weren't important because our son would be born dead anyway. I felt as if the hospital had abandoned us as our greatest hour of need quickly approached. I briefly made eye contact with our special nurse as she gave me a small smile from the corner of her mouth. She continued to assure me that everything would work out. I couldn't look at her, or speak to her, because I was so angry I didn't know if I would scream or cry, or both. I only knew I needed to be strong. As the contractions came, Kristine would pull herself together just enough to push, before falling back in complete exhaustion. The vicious cycle seemed to go on forever.

Kristine was giving up. She felt she couldn't go on any longer. Her body was so weak she could barely speak in a whisper. I tried my best, with the help of the nurse, to encourage her, and assure her that she was almost there. Our son was going to be born, soon. Almost two hours of pushing had drained every last ounce of energy that Kristine had. Our son had now been in the birth canal for over an hour and finally his head was ready to crown. I looked around the room; we were still alone. I knew my son was already dead.

Five and a half months had passed since we first found out there was something wrong. Now as I watched the birth process progress, I could see the dark hair on my son's head. I now knew within the hour that it would all be over. I had prepared myself as best I could for the journey to this moment, but I had not prepared for, or truly thought about the reality of this moment. Fear overwhelmed me, as I stood alone. To this point the whole pregnancy seemed to be something surreal, never coming to a conclusion, as if chasing a rainbow. Somehow I failed to foresee the physical climax of the birth. I was nauseous and faint. My physical and emotional strength drained out through this huge hole of unexpected truth; there would be a birth. I now understood the fear that Kristine carried throughout the pregnancy. I beg her forgiveness for not sharing its cross sooner.

Irony exploded in my face when the hospital room door flung open and the doctor walked in. The physician on duty at that critical time was none other than the doctor, who at our first visit to the high-risk office, had attacked our faith and pushed for an abortion. We had been through so much already I didn't care who we had as a doctor. I had given up. The doctor turned to the support staff that followed close behind and waved them off with a gesture I assumed meant they were not needed. I knew my son was going to be dead upon delivery, although I still held out a glimmer of hope for a miracle. God could still suspend the natural law and correct this error of nature. The only people present in our room were the doctor, a neonatologist, two nurses, including our special nurse, Kristine and I. A priest, we were told, was waiting outside in the hall.

XV

Against All Odds

Watching my son's head crowning, and then coming forth during the birth process, was amazing and beautiful. I was stunned to see a perfect little head: covered in long dark hair like my own. His head appeared normal to me. I stood in shock at the realization of a little baby boy. I had never pictured in my mind an image of what he may have looked like. I had only retained the snowy black and white images of the sonograms. I felt so sorry for what this little guy had to suffer. Anger and grief were overcoming my senses as my son became real to me. A cold shiver of loneliness quickly swept over me, forcing me to tremble.

Our son's head had easily made it through the birth process; however, his birth defect was hindering his body from completing the delivery; the doctor had to perform an episiotomy. One good strong push from Kristine enabled the doctor to help our son be born. Kristine let out an ear piercing scream, and then a sigh of relief. Witnessing Francis' birth painted a vivid scene upon my mind that will never fade. The image lasted but a couple quick seconds. The doctor had removed Francis from the womb with one hand while cutting the umbilical cord with the other. Francis was hurriedly placed into the hands of the neonatologist. Kristine never saw the birth because the nurse had used Kristine's legs, which were up in stirrups, along with a blanket, to create a temporary curtain. I believe it was a blessing she did not see Francis at the moment of his birth.

I never saw Francis' face during the birth process. He was either face down or twisted to the side away from me. The gruesome sonograms had revealed the truth. Francis had a major birth defect. A grotesque mass, that appeared larger than his body, was protruding from where his chest and abdomen should have been. His coloration was uneven shades of gray. His

34

head was a darkish gray, while his arms, which fell with gravity, looked white. The misshapen mass was a shiny dark brown color, almost like the color of a liver. His legs were a dull gray and were contorted up alongside the protruding mass. It was all I could do to take in what I did during that brief moment. The sight of his birth tempted me to hide in disgust.

There was no slap of hand on skin. The cry of a newborn was not heard. Francis was placed on the infant exam table by the neonatologist, the bright light shining down on him. Kristine was straining to see her newborn son, and yet I shielded her eyes. I told her to wait until the nurses could wrap him in a blanket. She kept asking if he was alive. The room remained silent as the medical staff cared for Kristine. She asked me what his birth defect was like. I told her to wait a few minutes and the nurse would wrap him so she could hold him. I continued to shield her eyes from this disturbing sorrow. Our son, Francis, after having come so far against all odds, appeared to be stillborn.

I watched the neonatologist moving the mass around, trying to find a position where it would be out of the way. I watched the doctor work to straighten his twisted legs. The doctor was working to place a diaper on Francis to contain the mass. A nurse was sent out of the room to retrieve a larger diaper. Kristine was still in the stirrups while the medical doctor catered to her complications. Kristine's placenta had dislodged and ruptured into many pieces during the delivery. She had lost a tremendous amount of blood. My focus was now on my wife who clung to a semiconscious state. I kept telling her it was finally all over; everything was going to be okay. She was fighting to stay alert; fighting, I feared, for her life.

XVI

Caught Off Guard

Five minutes or more had now elapsed since Francis' birth. Suddenly the neonatologist spoke out, softly at first, then loud and clear 'He's alive, he's alive!' Everyone turned towards Francis. Out of the dead silence now in the room, pandemonium instantly erupted. Kristine shouted for someone to get the priest. She screamed at me to get the holy water we had brought. The doctors began giving orders to the nurses. Just as I saw the holy water bottle on the windowsill, the two nurses collided together out front of me, blocking my path. Kristine continued to call for the priest. I stood frozen amidst five seconds of chaos brought on by a totally unexpected surprise. It seemed everyone was caught off guard.

I heard the door to the hospital room swiftly burst open, followed by the unmistakable rustle of heavy cloth. I turned to see the familiar brown robe of a Franciscan Friar coming towards me. Someone handed him the holy water as he approached the exam table that held Francis. I met him at the exam table, where I got my first good look at my newborn son. The light shone down brightly on Francis and his birth defect. He was laid bare, for the whole world to see. I could barely look at him. I felt embarrassed for my son. 'What is the child's name?' the priest asked. I could barely muster a response; 'Francis, his name is Francis, after St. Francis of Assisi.' The good friar then proceeded to baptize my son. He blessed Francis, and then quickly left the room. The doctors immediately wrapped Francis so we could hold him!

The enormous weight that we had been under was at once thrown off by the baptism. The atmosphere in the room changed instantaneously. I changed dramatically. Heavenly peace had descended upon us. I then remembered that earlier that morning in the waiting room, I had demanded, sinfully in my heart, a sign of miraculous wonder. I wanted a sign that would destroy all the doubt that I had been harboring. I wanted a sign that I could not question. I had needed to know that what we were doing was right. Then, as I watched the Franciscan leave the room, I realized that God had very subtly given me the greatest sign of all. God allowed this Franciscan, whom I did not know worked at the hospital, to be present at the perfect moment; to baptize a child named in faith, after the founder of his order. These events came together so beautifully for me that I truly recognized the presence of God among us at that moment.

Three diapers were used to contain the mass protruding from Francis' torso. A warm receiving blanket was carefully wrapped around his little body, allowing only his face and hands to be visible. Our special nurse handed my son to me. All activity in the room had ceased. I walked the few feet to Kristine's side struggling for every step. Emotions had gotten the better of me. I could not gather enough strength to utter even a sound. I literally could not speak. I became terrified at the thought that my son would die before I could tell him that I loved him. I had been the strong one throughout the pregnancy. Cold shivers rushed through my body like a raging torrent. Now, at the most crucial time of all, I found myself silenced.

XVII

A Perfect Soul

I presented my son to his mother, to the woman who had just endured a grueling twenty-seven hours of induced labor. Kristine sat up on the delivery bed and cuddled her newborn son in her arms. She lovingly gazed down upon her son, and then spoke slowly in a loud and clear voice,

"Oh Francis, I love you so much. I've waited so long to hold you. You are so beautiful... Jesus is here. The Blessed Mother is here. They've come to take you with them. You are going to a much better place. I love you! "

Kristine leaned over and expressed her love with a gentle kiss on his tiny forehead. I looked around the room and witnessed just how powerful a moment it was. Everyone present was in tears, including the doctor who had told us to have an abortion. She was leaning back against a wall, wearing bloodied gloves and an apron, trying to wipe her tears with her elbows. Kristine was enveloped in the light of God's grace. We could only stand back in the shadows and watch. I will forever revere that moment as the greatest manifestation of love from a mother for her child.

Our special nurse asked me if we would like her to clear the room so we could be alone with our son. I nodded yes, as I still could not speak, and everyone quickly left the room. Kristine and I finally were able to hold the child we had wanted so dearly. Together, we watched his little tongue moving. It appeared to me that he was doing his best to try to nurse. He never opened his eyes. He never cried. His occasional movements seemed to be merely involuntary spasms. We caressed his tiny little hands; noticing that one of them was slightly deformed. Two of his fingers, the pinkie and ring finger, had never separated, and had grown to only about half size. We realized that that was the hand that flashed us the peace sign, to let us know everything was going to be okay, at the very first sonogram so long ago. He was no longer hidden from us. Tears of joy and grief streamed down our faces as we marveled at how his dark hair and facial features resembled our own. Time stood still as we held our son.

I called for the nurse when it became apparent to me that Kristine was on the verge of passing out. As the hospital staff once again entered the room, Kristine kissed Francis on the forehead and motioned for me to take him. I cradled my son as I backed away from the commotion settling around his beautiful mother. I embraced him with the most powerful feelings of love and peace I had ever experienced. I could sense that his time was drawing near. I watched as his cute little baby tongue moved one last time; and then it stopped. The child that we loved so dear, and suffered so much for, had died in my arms. A perfect soul had entered Heaven! Amen! His time of birth was recorded as 1:00 P.M., his time of death was recorded as 1:20 P.M. We had just spent twenty minutes in eternity!

People had often asked me during the pregnancy if I had given any thought about what my child might have to suffer. I had thought about it, deeply. I knew that it was only through suffering, participation in the cross, that we could regain that which Adam had lost. As I look back in retrospect I can see the suffering my son endured in a clearer light. While carrying His cross along the Via Dolorosa, Christ met his Blessed Mother. How she must have held Him, if only for a moment, while he suffered. Later, upon the cross, Christ commended His Spirit into the hands of His Father. He suffered in His mother's arms, and died in His father's hands. Francis too, had suffered in his mother's arms, and then died in his father's hands. There could not have been any other way for my son to pass.

Francis was clothed with the white baptismal garment we had chosen. We held our son's body knowing that a perfect soul, a saint, was now watching over us from Heaven. I have no regrets about anything that occurred throughout the pregnancy. I have seen its fruition. Though I will always carry a deep sorrow in my heart over the loss of my son, I will hold a more powerful joy in knowing he is with Christ. We held Francis's body close, and made sure to take some pictures together. Finally we gave up his mortal remains, to be covered with a receiving blanket, and taken out of the room. Kristine fell back exhausted into a much-needed sleep.

The hospital asked permission to conduct an autopsy on Francis' remains. Francis, we felt, had been through enough. I did not want my son to be gawked over, and taken apart, like a high school science project. We denied the autopsy request. We did, however, give a geneticist, who had driven from out of state after hearing of the birth, permission to study Francis as he was, and to take a few x-rays. That night the geneticist informed Kristine that he believed a blood clot had lodged in Francis' developing body even before she knew she was pregnant. The doctor sent us a copy of his detailed report and summary several months later. A small, simple blood clot, during the first weeks of pregnancy, had taken our son.

We had a simple funeral for our son. Fr. Robert, who always preached without a script, gave a fitting and moving homily. The church's cantor, a personal friend, obliged our wishes and played every verse of every hymn we had chosen. We were thankful for the support we received from all those present; and hurt by those close to us who were missing. The reality of the situation, even after leaving the cemetery, took some time to sink in. The funeral, in its own way, was the last station along our way of the cross.

Words cannot begin to describe the deep feelings of pain and loss that accompanied those first few weeks after we returned home. We had dreamt of having a new baby in our house. We had been through so much only to return home empty handed. We were left to fondle a few precious memories rather than our newborn son. On the advice of my wife's cousin, we had saved in a special box, every card, letter, or any other item that was connected to Francis. We hold dear the first hat the nurse put on him, his hand and foot prints, and greatest of all, our own first class relic; a lock of his long dark hair.

God had truly blessed us. He gave us a son, and also the knowledge that our son was with Him forever. Francis is with us now in a greater way than he ever could have been on Earth. He has a special place in our family's heart where we visit him daily. Francis, our son, we love you very much! Pray for us!

XVIII

Expected News

The fall of 1999 brought us some wonderful, expected news. Almost one and a half years after Francis's death, we found out Kristine was pregnant again. Everyone thought we were crazy. People thought we were trying to replace the child we lost. The truth is that we had accepted what happened to Francis and were continuing on with our lives. Kris and I had always wanted more children and felt we were both ready to have another baby. Our child was expected to be born on June 30, 2000.

The moment we found out Kris was pregnant, we consecrated the pregnancy to St. Girard Majella, patron saint of expectant mothers and children. During our family prayer time, we would pray a chaplet invoking the saint's intersession. The whole family wore the saint's medal, or carried it on their person. His prayer cards and devotional pamphlets were scattered throughout our home and used daily. We would not be alone for this pregnancy.

One thing we learned from the last pregnancy was to place everything into God's hands. He will not fail us. Sometimes things may not go as we expect, but in the end He is always there. This is the attitude we tried to maintain over the next nine months. Be assured, we were very nervous going forward. We had been told that we had a small chance of the same thing happening again. We tried not to think about it. Kristine was scheduled for frequent sonograms to monitor the baby more closely. We were relieved after each sonogram to hear that everything was going well with our child. Kristine, of course, was a different story. She was watched very closely for any signs of preeclampsia throughout the pregnancy. We knew that at any time our situation could become serious.

Losing a child at birth makes you realize just how special a healthy child, and pregnancy, really is. Kristine and I knew first hand just how fragile a pregnancy could be, and for that reason we did not presume the outcome of this pregnancy. We didn't start preparing materially for the baby until the later months of the pregnancy. We took the pregnancy one day at a time and left all the shadows of our past burdens in God's hands.

XIX

A Sign from Heaven

I purchased a statue of St. Girard for Kristine. We kept the statue on the nightstand near our bed. We had given this pregnancy over to his care and we wanted a reminder to invoke him each morning and night. Just having the image of the great saint close by had an overall calming effect. Kristine had read a biography of St. Girard in the early weeks of the pregnancy. She was struck by the quantity of miracles the saint performed. She read with awe about his handkerchief, which after his death, was used to cure people simply by touching them with it. I decided I would try and locate a relic of this great saint to help give us strength throughout the coming months. Kristine promised St. Girard that somehow she would name the baby after him if everything turned out okay in the end.

One day while grocery shopping, Kristine happened to meet a retired priest from our area, Fr. Norman Cormier, whom we had started a friendship with during the last pregnancy. Every time he saw Kristine, while she was pregnant with Francis, he went out of his way to bless her and the baby. It did not matter when or where, if he noticed her, he blessed her. We had not informed anyone that Kristine was pregnant again, and yet Fr. Cormier noticed that special glow, and knew. He was thrilled to see that Kristine was expecting again. They chatted for a few minutes in the grocery aisle, and then parted with the usual blessing.

A couple weeks later we received an unexpected letter from Fr. Cormier. We were surprised because we normally only had contact with him at church functions. He stated in his letter that he had been thinking about us a lot after meeting Kristine in the grocery store that day. Fr. Cormier wrote that he had a strong desire to pray for our child and us. His desire to pray, and to pray alone, caused him to get in his car, spontaneously, and drive for over five hours to Quebec, Canada, to the Shrine of St. Anne de Beaupre. Arriving at the shrine, he went straight to the convent of the Sisters of St. Girard and prayed the rosary with them, offering it for our intentions. He said he stayed there the weekend praying for us.

Fr. Cormier enclosed a prayer card of St. Girard with his letter. He also wrote that he wanted us to have a relic of the great saint. He obtained a relic from the sisters and mailed it to us enclosed in the letter. I had goose bumps going up and down my arms. It was amazing. He did not know we wanted to obtain a relic. He did not know we had consecrated the pregnancy to St. Girard. On the spur of the moment he was motivated to drive alone to Canada and to pray for us. This was truly a sign from Heaven!

XX

A Very Special Day

On May 26, 2000, Kristine went to the doctor's office for her regular visit. She had been on bed rest for over four weeks, having developed preeclampsia at the thirtieth week of the pregnancy. The doctors were trying to buy some time and allow the child to develop its lungs. Kristine's protein level in her urine had spiked tremendously high that day. Her blood pressure was very high as well. The baby was still not due for about five weeks. An amniocentesis was performed to test if the child's lungs were developed enough to sustain its life. The amnio was positive; the child's lungs were adequately developed. Our doctor informed us that we needed to induce the pregnancy before anything serious happened to Kristine or the baby. Kristine became very scared. What would be the outcome of this pregnancy?

Once again we opted to try a natural birth rather than a cesarean section. Though there were many risks, our doctors were behind us. We made sure that we had our relic of St. Girard, a bottle of holy water, and several prayer booklets on hand. Kristine was admitted to the hospital the afternoon of May 26, 2000. That weekend the hospital was crowded with expectant mothers in a variety of serious conditions. Kristine was placed on watch for a couple days while the more serious cases were attended to. For two days we waited in the hospital room reliving memories, waiting for this new induction to begin.

On the morning of May 28th, 2000, the doctors began the induction. It proceeded slowly but surely into the night. Kristine by no means had it any easier this time around. That night she had a horrible reaction to a medication; given to control her nausea. Her body convulsed and contorted, along with a high fever and nausea, for over four hours. The nurses slowed the induction, and after the reaction had subsided, allowed Kristine to sleep until morning.

May 29th, 2000, the two-year anniversary of the birth and death of our son Francis found us once again in the middle of a serious pregnancy. That morning I prayed to my son to watch over his mother and new sibling. I told him to honor his mother and not allow anything to happen to her or the new baby. In the back of my mind I thought that this new baby might be born today; I prayed the child would not die that day. I did feel safe knowing I had my son Francis looking down over us, on what I considered his feast day.

As the hour of Francis's birth approached, Kristine showed no signs of imminent delivery, She was not dilating, and the contractions were few and far between. Our doctor had left for the day and would check in on us later that night. We talked about how wonderful it would have been to have this child born on Francis' day. Soon after we discussed these thoughts, Kristine's contractions began getting stronger and longer, and suddenly, her water broke.

She was starting to dilate. The doctor was called back to the hospital. Everything moved very quickly over the next few hours. The doctor said Kristine would deliver that night. Around 5:45 that afternoon, the doctor found Kristine was fully dilated. Kristine now had the urge to start pushing. The doctor called to have a special delivery room prepared. She didn't want to take any chances, as the baby was five weeks premature. She told Kristine not to push until she gave the okay.

The urge became too great as Kristine was wheeled into the special delivery room. The doctor didn't even have a chance to suit up and put rubber gloves on, when Kristine began to push. The delivery had begun. Three strong pushes later our fourth child, a little girl, was born. She was beautiful. Born on her brother's anniversary. I held her tight after the delivery while the staff attended to Kristine, who once again had some minor complications. Tears welled up in my eyes as I looked at my special little girl.

We named her Rachel Anne, after St. Anne, the mother of Our Lady. We had promised to somehow name this child after St. Girard. We decided that naming her after St. Anne, whom St. Girard had a strong devotion to, would fulfill our promise. St. Girard, I am sure, understands. We also told St. Girard that he could call our daughter Rachel to be one of the Sisters of St. Girard, and we would be honored. I thank this great saint, and my son, Francis, for their help. I thank God for my beautiful and healthy baby girl, Rachel.

May 29th is a very special day in our lives. We have a son in heaven, and now a wonderful little girl bound together eternally on that day. Rachel's older brother was watching out for her. The Lord had decided to bless our entire family that day with a tremendous gift of love. May 29th will never be just a coincidence to us; it will be a reminder of God's love for us.

Author's Note

On the day of Francis's funeral, Fr. Robert, our spiritual director for over three years, was scheduled to be at the hospital early in the morning for special tests. Unknown to us, he had not been feeling well. He decided to be late for his appointment in order to be the celebrant at our son's funeral. Fr. Robert began suffering greatly from an undiagnosed illness from that time on. The disease proved to be terminal. After battling the illness for over a year, Fr. Robert passed away on August 16, 1999. Fr. Robert gave me one last bit of spiritual direction just before he died. I will leave it with you…

"Please don't ever let any human event erase, or fade, the experience of God's manifestation of His love for you."

Amen.